Take Charge, Snoopy

Charles M. Schulz

Selected cartoons from
KISS HER YOU BLOCKHEAD!
Volume 1

CORONET BOOKS
Hodder and Stoughton

PEANUTS Comic Strips by Charles M. Schulz

Copyright © 1982 by United Features Syndicate

First published in the United States of America in 1984 by Ballantine Books

Coronet edition 1986

British Library C.I.P.

Schulz, Charles M.
    Take charge, Snoopy : selected cartoons from Kiss her you blockhead! Volume 1.
    1. American wit and humor, Pictorial
    I. Title
    741.5'973   NC1429

    ISBN 0–340–37888–3

Printed and bound in Great Britain for Hodder and Stoughton Paperbacks, a division of Hodder and Stoughton Ltd., Mill Road, Dunton Green, Sevenoaks, Kent (Editorial Office: 47 Bedford Square, London, WC1 3DP) by Cox & Wyman Ltd., Reading

Take Charge, SNOOPY

BONK!

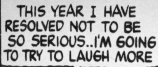

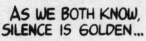

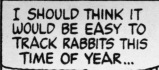

I SHOULD THINK IT WOULD BE EASY TO TRACK RABBITS THIS TIME OF YEAR...

THERE MUST BE A LOT OF THEM AROUND HERE

WHAT WOULD YOU DO RIGHT NOW IF YOU SAW A RABBIT?

HIT HIM WITH A SNOWBALL!

THERE'S A RABBIT! SEE HIM? OVER THERE!

ARE YOU GOING TO TRY TO HIT HIM WITH A SNOWBALL?

THROWING SNOWBALLS AT RABBITS IS RISKY...

THEY THROW BACK!

SCHULZ

WHICH DO YOU THINK LASTS LONGER IN LIFE, THE GOOD THINGS OR THE BAD THINGS?

GOOD THINGS LAST EIGHT SECONDS.. BAD THINGS LAST THREE WEEKS

WHAT ABOUT IN BETWEEN?

IN BETWEEN YOU SHOULD TAKE A NAP...

AS SOON AS THIS GROUND IS SPADED, I'M GOING TO ORGANIZE MY GARDEN

I'M GOING TO PLANT POTATOES, AND BEANS, AND RADISHES AND PEAS

WHY ARE YOU TELLING ME ALL THIS?

OH!

OKAY, HIRED HAND... HERE'S WHAT I WANT YOU TO DO...

I NEED THIS WHOLE YARD SPADED SO I CAN PLANT MY GARDEN..

ARE YOU SURE YOU'VE DONE THIS KIND OF WORK BEFORE?

WHAT ARE YOU GUYS DOING?

WE'RE HELPING LUCY PLANT HER GARDEN... FIRST WE SPADED IT.. NOW WE'RE PLANTING IT...

ACTUALLY, WE JUST DO WHAT WE'RE TOLD..

WELL, IT LOOKS VERY NICE... WHAT ARE YOU PLANTING?

FRENCH FRIES

HERE, HIRED HAND..TAKE THESE PACKAGES OF SEEDS OUT TO THE GARDEN...

THE PHONE'S RINGING..I'LL BE OUT IN A MINUTE TO SHOW YOU WHAT TO DO...

I'M SORRY, I CAN'T TALK TO YOU NOW...MY HIRED HAND AND I ARE PLANTING MY GARDEN...

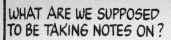

HOW MANY TREES HAVE YOU WRITTEN DOWN?

OAK, POPLAR, SPRUCE, APPLE, MAPLE, PINE, CEDAR AND BIRCH... THAT MAKES EIGHT...

I'VE ONLY GOT ONE..

"FALLEN"

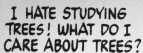

EVEN THOUGH YOU GOT ALL THE ANSWERS WRONG WHEN YOU WERE UP AT THE BLACKBOARD, SIR, I WAS PROUD OF YOU!

YOU WERE PROUD OF ME, MARCIE?

ABSOLUTELY, SIR

YOU SHOWED A LOT OF POISE!

They could never agree on anything.

"Why don't we truck on down to the bike shop?" she asked.

"No," he said. "Let's bike on down to the truck shop."

Their marriage counselor was not at all encouraging.

HEY, PARTNER, IT'S ME, MOLLY VOLLEY!

?

THERE'S A MIXED DOUBLES TENNIS TOURNAMENT THIS WEEK...I HOPE YOU'RE IN GOOD SHAPE...

I KNOW I'VE GAINED WEIGHT, BUT IF YOU SAY ANYTHING, I'LL HIT YOU OVER THE HEAD WITH MY RACKET!

WHEN I KNOW I COULD GET HIT OVER THE HEAD WITH A RACKET, I CAN BE THE SOUL OF DISCRETION!

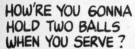

LOOK WHO WE PLAY IN THE FIRST ROUND... "CRYBABY" BOOBIE AND "BAD CALL" BENNY!

BOOBIE COMPLAINS ABOUT EVERYTHING, AND BENNY CALLS EVERYTHING "OUT"!

I REMEMBER THE LAST TIME I PLAYED AGAINST HIM...

AS SOON AS I OPENED THE CAN OF BALLS, HE CALLED THEM "OUT"!

WHAT'S GOING ON?

IT'S THE FIRST ROUND OF THE MIXED DOUBLES TENNIS TOURNAMENT

SNOOPY AND MOLLY VOLLEY ARE PLAYING "CRYBABY" BOOBIE AND "BAD CALL" BENNY!

SEE? THEY'RE JUST INTRODUCING THEMSELVES NOW..I IMAGINE THEY'RE BEING VERY POLITE...

WELL, IF IT ISN'T "FAT LEGS" VOLLEY!!

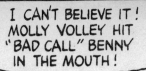

I CAN'T BELIEVE IT! MOLLY VOLLEY HIT "BAD CALL" BENNY IN THE MOUTH!

NOBODY CALLS ME "FAT LEGS," KID!!

YOU HIT MY PARTNER IN THE MOUTH!

SHUT UP, "CRYBABY"!

OH, TO BE AT WIMBLEDON NOW THAT SPRING IS HERE...

Dear Son,

Thank you for considering us with your letter.

We regret, however, that it does not suit our present needs. Sincerely, Mother

EVEN MY LETTERS HOME GET REJECTED!

A "SUMMER READING LIST.." WHAT'S A "SUMMER READING LIST"?

OUR TEACHER HOPES WE'LL DO SOME READING DURING SUMMER VACATION

THESE ARE BOOKS SHE HAS SUGGESTED WE READ JUST FOR PLEASURE...

FOR **WHAT?**

TWO WEEKS AT "BEANBAG" CAMP! NOTHING TO DO FOR TWO WEEKS EXCEPT LIE IN A BEANBAG! THIS IS GONNA BE PERFECT!

GOODBYE, BIG BROTHER.. I'LL WRITE IF THEY GIVE US TIME...

DON'T WORRY ABOUT IT! JUST RELAX, AND ENJOY YOURSELF...

IS THIS THE LINE FOR THE BUS?

WHO'S PUSHING?

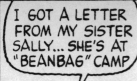

ALL RIGHT, TROOPS, I HAVE A QUESTION FOR YOU...

HAS ANY OF YOU EVER READ A COMPASS?

"NO, BUT I READ THE REVIEWS"

I HATE JOKES LIKE THAT!

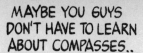

MAYBE YOU GUYS DON'T HAVE TO LEARN ABOUT COMPASSES..

I'VE HEARD THAT BIRDS HAVE SORT OF A BUILT-IN COMPASS SO THAT THEIR BRAINS TELL THEM WHICH WAY TO GO

MAYBE YOU GUYS HAVE A NATURAL SENSE OF DIRECTION

BUT I DOUBT IT!

SCHULZ

I GOT ANOTHER LETTER FROM MY SISTER SALLY

"I AM STILL ENJOYING 'BEANBAG' CAMP...ALL WE DO IS LIE IN OUR BEANBAGS, WATCH TV AND EAT JUNK FOOD

"SOMETIMES THEY SHOW US OLD MOVIES"

I'LL BET "ROSEBUD" TURNS OUT TO BE HIS SLED!

THAT'S RIGHT... SALLY COMES HOME TODAY FROM "BEANBAG" CAMP

I'LL BE INTERESTED TO SEE IF SHE'S CHANGED...

ALL THEY DO THERE IS LIE IN THEIR BEANBAGS, WATCH TV AND EAT JUNK FOOD...

I'M HOME!

ALSO AVAILABLE FROM CORONET BOOKS

CHARLES M. SCHULZ
Peanuts

All these books are available at your local bookshop or newsagent, or can be ordered direct from the publisher. Just tick the titles you want and fill in the form below.

Prices and availability subject to change without notice.

CORONET BOOKS, P.O. Box 11, Falmouth, Cornwall.

Please send cheque or postal order, and allow the following for postage and packing:

U.K. – 55p for one book, plus 22p for the second book, and 14p for each additional book ordered up to a £1.75 maximum.

B.F.P.O. and EIRE – 55p for the first book, plus 22p for the second book, and 14p per copy for the next 7 books, 8p per book thereafter.

OTHER OVERSEAS CUSTOMERS – £1.00 for the first book, plus 25p per copy for each additional book.

Name ....

Address ....

....